WITHDRAWN

DATE DUE			
NOV 30 1970			
JAN 21 1971	NOV 11 1985		
MAR 5 1971	OCT 27 1987		
JUL 8 1971	FEB 7 1990		
JAN 27 1972	FEB 11 1992		
	DEC 30 1998		
	DEC 14 2001		
FEB 13 1979			
JAN 23 1980			
DEC 5 1989			
APR 9 1990			
DEC 24 1980			
GAYLORD			PRINTED IN U.S.A.

SMALL GAME

Animals of the Americas

by C.B. Colby

Coward-McCann, Inc.   **New York**

Small Game of the Americas

As with the big animals you may have seen in my book *Big Game*, I have selected for *Small Game* the animals of which I could find the most interesting information and the best photographs. Some of the most interesting had to be omitted because they are so elusive that no photos are available nor can one find any amount of authentic information about their habits. Perhaps someday one of you may become a naturalist photographer and help fill the vacant spots in the file of photos now available.

Those that I have included from both North and South America as well as Central America and Mexico are typical of their kind. In almost every case there are other members of their family tree which are very similar in appearance, habits and range, so I have selected from a particular species those members of which I could obtain the best photos and information.

In some cases these photos had to be of animals in zoological gardens rather than in the wild because of the rarity of the animal. Although all of us dislike seeing wildlife restrained, the animals in zoos are often better off than those on the outside, for their health is guarded by experienced veterinarians and as far as possible their natural food and habitat are reproduced for their health and comfort. As a matter of unpleasant fact, the animals you enjoy seeing and watching in zoological parks might have been destroyed by accident or their natural enemies long ago had they *not* been captured and saved for your education. In the zoo, you can watch them at close range in perfect safety. Without zoological parks very few animals from distant countries would ever be seen except by those who also live there.

Some of the small game animals you will see on the following pages may be native to your area and you can observe them yourselves if you know where to look for them, and have the patience to find them. Check with your state conservation department, or local sportsmen who generally know where game is to be found. If your city has a zoo, or if you travel on your vacation to an area where there is one, you may want to pay it a visit. Learning about our wildlife, even some of the small animals you will meet on the following pages, will give you not only pleasure, but a new knowledge of some of the wild neighbors who may live closer than you think.

Even here where I live, less than fifty miles from Times Square in New York City, there are foxes, raccoons, opossums, woodchucks, muskrat, mink, otter, and occasionally even a bobcat, not to mention squirrels, rabbits, weasels and chipmunks. If you live near a few acres of woodland, fields, or pond or stream, chances are you too have one or more of these interesting neighbors right nearby. Go and look for them.

I would like to thank the many zoo officials who gave me their friendly cooperation in helping me get these fine photos. In particular I would like to thank Mrs. Beatrice Boone, Photographic Librarian of the Office of Conservation Education, U. S. Fish and Wildlife Service, Department of the Interior, and Mrs. Dorothy Reville, Photographic Librarian of the New York Zoological Society, of which I am a member. My thanks too, for the cooperation of some of the critters themselves who let me get close enough to photograph them and get to know them without objecting too emphatically to my curiosity. The help of these fine folks (of all species) made this book one of the most pleasant of all those I have worked on.

—C. B. Colby

Bureau of Sport Fisheries and Wildlife, U. S. Department of Interior photographers E. P. Hadden, Robert D. Jones Jr., V. P. Scheffer, Walter P. Taylor, Luther C. Goldman, and Peter J. Van Huizen: pages 2, 3, 5, 7, 10, 14, 17, 22, 23, 25, 27, and title page; National Park Service, U. S. Department of Interior photographer Joseph F. Dixon: 21; Saskatchewan Government: 26; National Zoological Park, Smithsonian Institution: 42; New York State Conservation Department Division of Conservation Education: 24; Author, full-color cover and 6; New York Zoological Society: 4, 8, 9, 11, 12, 13, 15, 16, 18, 19, 20, 28, 29, 30, 31, 32, 33, 34, 35, 36, 37, 38, 39, 40, 41, 42, 43, 44, 45, 46, 47, 48. 08 up

© 1968 by C. B. Colby. All rights reserved. Printed in the United States of America.
Library of Congress Catalog Card Number: 68-23858

This rare photo shows a sea otter sleeping in a bed of kelp where it goes for safety from its natural enemy, the killer whale.

Contents

Small Game of the Americas	3	Snowshoe Rabbit	26
Gray Wolf	4	Virginia Opossum	27
Coyote	5	Bobcat	28
Red Fox	6	Canada Lynx	29
Arctic Fox	7	Kinkajou	30
Eastern Gray Fox	8	Nine-banded Armadillo	31
Raccoon	9	Great and Six-banded Armadillo	32
Ring-tailed Cat	10	Agouti	33
Coatimundi	11	Capybara	34
Porcupine	12	Tree Porcupine	35
Beaver	13	Northern Giant Otter	36
Muskrat	14	Chinchilla	37
Nutria	15	Jaguarundi	38
River Otter	16	Ocelot	39
Sea Otter	17	Maned Wolf	40
Badger	18	Azara's Dog	41
Wolverine	19	Round-eared Dog	42
Woodchuck	20	Ecuadorian Wild Dog	43
Marmot	21	Bush Dog	44
Skunk	22	Tamandua	45
Javelina	23	Three-toed Sloth	46
Cottontail Rabbit	24	Two-toed Sloth	47
Jackrabbit	25	Tayra	48

Gray Wolf Canis lupus

One of the most interesting animals to be found anywhere is the wolf. This doglike animal is a member of the order Carnivora, the meat eaters. It lives on anything from mice to moose and occasionally domestic livestock. It is a social animal and the family is a close-knit unit, living and hunting together until the youngsters are old enough to start families of their own. They can weigh as much as 150 pounds, although the average is a little less. The males are heavier and larger than their mates. They range in color from gray to almost all black, except for the arctic species which is pure white. Black, gray and white wolves may be found in same territory. They are found in some parts of the continental United States, but are most abundant in Canada, Alaska and isolated areas of Mexico. They stand about 32 inches at shoulder and are about 4½ feet long. Tales of wolves attacking men are greatly exaggerated; actually such attacks are almost unknown. They live in underground dens or in caves. In winter several families join up for better hunting. About five to nine pups born in spring. Their eyes open in nine days and they are weaned in eight weeks. Wolves live for about 15 years. There is no more thrilling sound in the wilds than the howls of a pack of wolves on a moonlit night!

Coyote Canis latrans

Another of our smaller meat eaters is the coyote, also known as the prairie wolf or brush wolf. These members of the Carnivora order are smaller than wolves, averaging about 25 pounds in weight and standing about 28 inches at the shoulder. However, some have been taken weighing as much as 40 pounds. The males are larger of the two sexes and both male and female have larger ears than the wolves. They often hunt in relays to tire out a pursued animal, but seldom in troops or packs, as wolves do. They live on rodents, rabbits, carrion, fruit, and vegetables, with an occasional taste for livestock, particularly young lambs, colts and calves. They range from Central America to Alaska and as far east as New England, in the remote areas. Coyotes live to be about 14 years old. They usually mate for life and have litters of from four to six pups in the spring. Maximum size of litter is ten. Their color is usually brown, sprinkled with black and gray, though the overall color may vary from gray to brown. When running, coyotes carry their tails high rather than low, as the wolves do. The nose pads of coyotes are generally less than an inch wide, while those of a wolf are much wider—one way to identify a coyote from a wolf of the same size. The yapping high-pitched howl of the coyote is very different from the rising and falling chorus of a wild wolf pack.

Red Fox Vulpes fulva

The red fox can also be known as cross fox, silver fox, and black fox, for all of these color variations may be found in a single litter. The typical red fox is golden or reddish above with white underneath, a white tail tip and black legs. Young red foxes also have black on the muzzle and behind the ears. The cross fox is more reddish brown and the silver fox is all black with a white tail tip and silver or gray hairs on the back. Silver fox was once a very popular fur for women's coats. A typical red fox weighs about 15 pounds and stands about a foot high at the shoulder. They live on small rodents, poultry and birds, as well as grass, fruit and vegetables. They even take very young lambs and kids if available. They range over most of the North American continent from the Arctic to the tropics, often within a few miles of large cities. They live underground in dens called "earths," usually taken over from some other animal. One species known as the gray fox is smaller and is unique in that it often climbs trees in search of fruit and birds' nests. Red foxes have litters of from one to five, usually four. The male brings food to his mate and cubs for some weeks. Foxes can give off a strong odor like a skunk when greatly excited or frightened. They are intelligent animals and use all sorts of tricks to elude a pursuer.

Arctic Fox Alopex lagopus

Nature always adapts her youngsters to the areas in which they live. Arctic foxes are usually snow-white to match the snowy wastes in which they live. There is also a blue phase of this arctic fox which is shown in the photo above, taken on Gareloi Island in the Aleutian Islands of Alaska. These foxes are a bluish gray and are almost as difficult to see as the white members of the species, for they look like shadows against the snow. Note the pile of seabirds in the front of the animal's den in the coastal rocks. The arctic foxes live on birds, carrion, eggs, stranded fish and similar fare. They often follow polar bears to feed on what is left of seals the bears feed upon. These arctic foxes weigh about the same as the typical red fox and are about the same size. They vary slightly in size in different regions and the male is generally slightly larger than the female. They make their dens in rocky caves, or among the ice ridges of the Arctic. They are heavier than the red fox and in winter they develop a very heavy coat and grow hair on the bottoms of their feet for better travel on ice. Their ears are shorter and more rounded than those of the red fox. They have one to fourteen pups with about five surviving every spring. All foxes often store uneaten food. Some white arctic foxes turn brown in summer.

Eastern Gray Fox Urocyon cineroargenteus

Whoever heard of a fox climbing a tree? Well, this one does, and does it well and frequently. This gray fox is most often found in the eastern part of the United States, although it can be found over most of the states, in small areas. It is not as intelligent as the red fox and can be trapped easily. Its fur is of little value although some is used commercially. The gray fox is about 44 inches long including the tail and it weighs about 7 to 13 pounds. Its range overlaps the range of the red fox but generally it prefers the warmer states. It feeds on both meat and vegetation and, since it climbs trees so well, it can find fruit and in many cases birds and eggs. It has from one to seven pups in a litter, usually in early spring. They are usually born in dens dug in sandy banks. Both parents help take care of the youngsters and teach them to hunt until they can take care of themselves. This well-fed and happy gang of gray foxes is shown in their big outdoor enclosure at the famous New York Zoological Park, Bronx, New York.

Raccoon Procyon lotor

If the raccoons that I feed at my back door every night are typical of all of these masked bandits, they are about the cleverest sneak thieves alive. There is hardly a bolt, lock or latch that can stop them, and they can untie knots almost faster than a Boy Scout can tie them. These chunky ring-tailed animals can be found almost anywhere there is food of any kind, even within the city limits of big cities. They can weigh as much as 25 pounds and stand up to about 15 inches high. The average is usually lighter and smaller. Their color is usually a rich brown-gray but may be almost white. Their tails are ringed with brown and black and their eyes are "masked" with black. Their forepaws are nimble and strong and they are said to wash everything they eat. I have never been able to get "my" raccoons to do this, even when I furnish a pan of water. Their natural food is mainly aquatic: fish, frogs, crayfish, turtles, and shellfish. Perhaps because they fish for them with their paws, they are thought to be "washing" their catch. They are found over most of North America and into Mexico. They live in hollow trees, logs and sometimes caves. They have one to six young in late spring or summer and the family stays together for a year. They live about 13 years and, if caught young, make good pets.

Ring-tailed Cat Bassariscus astutus

Throughout our southwestern states and down into Mexico, the ring-tailed cat, civet, or cacomistle, whichever name you like best, wears one of the longest and fanciest tails of any small game animal. Of its average 2½ feet of length, over half is fancy black and white tail. It averages about 2½ pounds in weight. The ringtail spends most of the day sleeping in rocky dens or hollow trees. Its color is generally a yellowish brown, with light areas about its ears, eyes and muzzle. Like the coatimundi (a similar animal with a slightly ringed tail), the ringtail is related to the raccoon, also a nocturnal animal. The ringtail feeds on small mammals, small birds, insects and fruit, and has three to four young in May or June. It has a fondness for poultry. Yet the ringtail is so secretive that, even though it is known to be around henyards, it is seldom seen. The claws of this handsome little animal are semiretractile, while those of cats are fully retractile. Although it has few enemies owing to its night hunting, it is a favorite prey of the horned owl.

Coatimundi Nasua narica

Like the ring-tailed cat, opposite, this small game also has a splendidly long and ringed tail, although not nearly as stylish as that of the ringtail. This animal is found in the southwestern states, principally in Arizona, New Mexico and Texas, and has hind legs quite a bit longer than its front ones. It is about a foot high at the shoulder and, including its splendid tail, is about 50 inches long. Its color is reddish brown with lighter color on throat, chin and chest. The legs and feet are almost black and the tail is ringed with light and dark bands. Its long snout is very mobile, almost like a short trunk, and the small rounded ears are set quite far back on its head. Coatis weight about 25 pounds. They have an odd habit of being active both day and night, taking time off at noon and midnight for sleeping. They are expert climbers, using their long tails as a balance. They feed on fruit, vegetables, insects, worms, small animals and small birds. They have four to six young in a litter born in early summer. Similar species are found in Mexico and as far south as Peru. The animal shown is the dusky coati *(Nasua narica solitaria)*.

Porcupine Erethizon dorsatum

Contrary to popular legend and Longfellow's famous poem *Hiawatha,* the "porky" or "quill pig" cannot hurl its quills. But it can switch its tail like a flash and drive its quills into anything near it. The quills in the tail come out easily and are barbed, so they penetrate flesh deeply and work their way deeper unless removed at once. Porcupines weigh up to 40 pounds and can be found over most of the North American continent where there is heavy timber. Each animal has thousands of these "quills." They are actually not quills (the hollow stem of a feather) but modified hairs. About the only animal who can safely hunt and kill porcupines is the fisher, a big weasel which is very fast. Bears also have been known to kill them by scooping them up with a paw and hurling them against a tree or ledge. They are protected in some areas as they are the only animal a starving man can walk up to and kill for food. They do great damage to trees because they gnaw the bark for food, often staying a week in a single tree. They have one youngster at a time or occasionally twins. The little porkies can climb a tree when they are only two days old. Porcupines do not hibernate like chipmunks and raccoons (the latter only in really bad weather) or bears, but they do den up during a bad storm—taking shelter in hollow trees and logs. They are apt to gnaw anything that has a salty taste from perspiration, such as paddles, ax handles, hunting knives, canoe gunwales and seats.

Beaver Castor canadensis

The expression "busy as a beaver" is quite a compliment to anyone, for this animal is always on the go—building dams and houses, gathering food or repairing its various properties. Beaver are found in Canada in great numbers and in many parts of northern United States. They may weigh as much as 65 pounds but the average weight is about 30 pounds. Their fur is a glossy brown and very warm. Much of the wealth of early Canada came from the beaver pelts it produced. Beaver live in colonies of single families, including as many as a dozen old and young. Beaver mate for life and the family stays together for over a year or until the young wander off on their own. They live on the bark of aspen and willow trees, and store great piles of this wood underwater, anchored in the mud for winter use. Their homes are either lodges built of cleverly interwoven sticks and mud or dens in the bank of a stream. There is a central chamber above water level, a ventilating opening in the roof and often other rooms for the young. The house is secure against predators and the dam keeps water at a certain level. A leak in the dam is detected by dropping of water level and at once repaired. Beaver live almost 20 years and have from one to eight young in late spring.

Muskrat Ondatra zibethica

This little game animal has undoubtedly provided more country boys with spending money than any other small animal in the Americas. Muskrat have been hunted and trapped for their meat and fine soft hides ever since the days of the Pilgrims and many a young man has paid his way through school with their help. But their numbers are still undepleted. They can be found in almost any swampy or marshy spot. They build small domed grass and mud homes similar to those of the beaver but on a much smaller scale. The muskrat measures about 2 feet in length and weighs about 2 pounds. Its tail is about 10 inches long, scaly and sparsely haired. Its hind feet are webbed and it is an excellent swimmer. Muskrat feed on water plants, frogs, fish and freshwater mussels. They were known as the musquash to the Indians, who frequently used them for food. The white man never was enthusiastic over them as food. They have litters of four to eleven young, from three to five times a year. An average litter numbers from six to eight. Muskrat are found all over North America in fresh or saltwater marshland. They are our most common aquatic animal.

Nutria Nutria myocaster

The nutria is a sort of emigrant to the United States from South America. They are found naturally south of Peru on both sides of the Andes, but were introduced into the United States in 1930, to be raised for their fur. During a 1940 flood, hundreds were washed out of their pens and so became wild. They adopted their new country with gusto. Only eight years later over 50,000 were trapped on the lower Mississippi delta. They weigh about 20 pounds and are 3 feet long. Much of their fur is used in making felt. Like the muskrat and beaver, they have webbed hind feet, and they live on aquatic plants. They can have litters of from three to twelve young every four months the year around. The female has a unique feature—her nipples are along her back instead of her underside, so she can nurse her young while they both float in the water for safety. Nutrias are short-lived, the females living about 3 years and the males not much more than 6 years. They are also known in some areas as "river mice" or "mouse beavers" and are protected as fur-bearing animals in some areas of the country. This South American aquatic animal is now well established over many of our southern coastal areas.

River Otter Lutra canadensis

This amazing animal, also known as the Canadian otter, is one of the most graceful of all animals, whether in the water, on land or in action. They can be up to over 5 feet in length including a foot-long tail. The male, called a dog-otter, weighs up to 30 pounds while the female, called a bitch (as is a female dog), weighs about 10 pounds less than her mate. They have one litter each year of from two to five young at almost any time of the year. Although they are superb swimmers, the youngsters have to be coaxed by their mother to take that first dip. They live on fish, frogs, birds, small animals and some vegetation, including fruit. They are very friendly and playful and make fine pets. They often play with small pebbles, love to wrestle, and enjoy sliding downhill on wet mud or snow, often doing this for an hour at a time, in a whole group. They live in dens in stream banks. They are found over most of the United States and Canada and in a few small areas in Mexico. Their fur is of top quality and is used as a standard of 100 percent by which to grade other types of fur for durability. They live to be about 15 years old. There are several species of otter, including the giant Brazilian otter of the Amazon basin which measures over 6½ feet long (page 36).

Sea Otter Enhydra lutris

This aquatic member of the weasel family did much to open our west, for the value of its fine fur drew many pioneer trappers to the far west. It also drew the Russians across the Bering Strait and down the Alaskan coast, for its fur was the badge of Russian and Chinese royalty. One pelt sold for as much as $2,500. The sea otter was trapped almost into extinction by 1900. Rigid protection in 1912, when it was said to be too late, did save them. They are now plentiful again in some areas of California and Alaska, but are still protected. They can have young at any time of year and there is usually a single pup, but occasionally twins. They live on shellfish, sea urchins and some fish. They often place a flat stone on their chests and smash sea urchins on it to break them open for food. They can dive to 300 feet. They hide in kelp beds and seldom come ashore, sleeping floating on their backs, often with the young pups sleeping on top of them. Some of these beautiful animals weigh as much as 80 pounds. Their hind feet are broad and shaped like flippers, with fur on both sides. Their fur is the most valuable of any fur-bearing animal, and is known as Kamchatka beaver. The fur is dense, glossy and brownish black in color with a sprinkling of white-tipped hair. The chief natural enemy of the sea otter is the killer whale.

Badger Taxidea taxus

This typically western animal has more courage and fighting ability when attacked than almost any other animal its size. It weighs up to about 25 pounds, although the average badger weighs about 15 pounds. It is low-slung with short legs armed with powerful claws and has strong teeth. Its skin is so tough and loose that an enemy can't get a good grip. If hard pressed, it can also give off a skunk-like musk to discourage an attacker further. Badgers live in dry country and dig burrows easily. They dig so fast they can catch ground squirrels and prairie dogs underground. This ability also helps save them when they are being pursued by predators or dogs. They are a grizzly gray and black color with a white stripe running from the nose back over the head and down the back almost to the tail. They have black cheeks and black-rimmed ears. Their legs, feet and nose are also black. The young, three or four in number, are born during late spring, and usually set out on their own the next fall. Badgers feed on ground rodents, lizards, snails, insects, carrion, snakes, birds and eggs. Since they eat many pests, they do a lot of good. They can climb and swim, if they have to, but usually prefer the ground for hunting. They live about 14 years, at least in captivity. The badger is a quite vocal character in a mumbling sort of way. As it wanders about in search of food, it wheezes and grumbles like an old man used to living alone and not liking it.

Wolverine Gulo luscus

If you could class animals like humans, these would be the delinquents of the wilderness. Wolverines seem to have a desire to be disliked and at this they are a howling success, for every trapper, north woods cabin owner and settler hate them. They will kill and tear to shreds any animal they find in a trap, often following a trapline and destroying every catch. They will enter a cabin and completely destroy everything in sight. What they cannot eat they will befoul with skunklike scent. They fear nothing, and even bears and mountain lions will give them the right-of-way. They live on anything they can catch including deer, and will kill anything they meet. A wolverine can drag a carcass three times its own weight for a long distance over rough ground with ease. They range over most of Canada and can be still found in remote areas of some of our most northern states. They are almost 4 feet long and weigh up to about 40 pounds. Their color is a dark brown with a lighter brown band from shoulder down around hips and back to opposite shoulder. They have powerful claws and teeth, and a short bushy tail. They den in burrows underground, where the females have three to four young each summer. Their fur is used for parka hoods, as a man's breath will not collect on it as ice in cold weather.

Woodchuck Marmota monax

What country boy, in the eastern half of the United States, has not sneaked up on one of these big rodents with his trusty .22 rifle, or stumbled upon one in a clover patch? The woodchuck is even known as the "country boy's grizzly" owing to its popularity as a target. It does great damage in gardens, and its den holes often cause broken legs among horses and cattle. It weighs up to about 15 pounds but usual weight is 10 or 12 pounds. It is also known as the groundhog and even has its own "day" on February 2. Woodchucks dig very complicated underground dens with several openings. When one feeds, it is seldom very far from one of its doorways. Usually these doors are under a rock, stone wall, or tough old stump to make pursuit even harder. Their natural enemies are coyotes, dogs, foxes and hawks. Their young number from two to eight, born in midspring. They mate as soon as they come out of winter hibernation in March or April. They feed on grass and all sorts of cultivated vegetables. They especially like clover. They also eat insects, small rodents and even small birds. Their color is a grizzly brown-gray, although some are almost white and some very dark brown. They usually live alone.

Marmot Marmota caligata

What the woodchuck is to the eastern folks, the marmot is to those who live in our western states and Alaska. The yellow-bellied marmot is found farther south than its relative the hoary marmot, which is found in Canada and up into our most northern state of Alaska. Marmots usually live among the rocks where they build their dens for safety. They look like woodchucks, to which they are related, except that they are frequently larger, and the hoary marmot has quite a bit of light gray or white on its head and shoulders, hence the name. The yellow-bellied marmot has yellowish fur on its underside. Marmots live on grasses and soft plants. They live about 13 years. They bear from two to five young in late spring. The young leave home within a few months, although some stay in the same den with their mother through their first winter. One of their characteristics is a sharp whistle when they spot an intruder in their home territory. This is evidently meant as a warning to their companions, but often it seems to be in defiance of an enemy, for they can vanish into their rocky tunnels and dens in a flash.

Skunk Mephitis mephitis

The striped skunk is too familiar to require lengthy descriptions. Everyone knows about the "black and white animal with the bushy tail" from photos, cartoons, or personal experiences. This member of the weasel family usually weighs about 10 pounds and measures about 30 inches long, including its bushy tail. Its color is always black and white but the areas of black and white may vary greatly. Some are almost all white, some almost all black. The typical striped skunk has a white line from its nose to the top of its head where it is all white; then the stripe divides and runs down both flanks of the animal to the tail where it may cover the whole tail or just the edges. Out west there is a smaller spotted skunk known as the "spilogale" (*Spilogale putorius*) which has short bars of white all over its neck and back and sides. It has a black tail with a white tip. Skunks are armed with a powerful and overpowering scent that can be shot accurately for up to 12 feet. They usually stamp their feet before "firing." They live on mice, insects, grubs, birds' eggs, and lizards. They even eat snakes. The young number from two to ten and are born in early summer. The spotted skunk can climb and swim well. Both species den in logs, under barns and buildings. They range over all of North America and down into Mexico.

Javelina Tayassu tajacu

Known by such names as collared peccary, javelina or musk hog, this small swine is found from Arizona, Texas and New Mexico as far south as Paraguay and southern Brazil. The peccary differs from the true pig in several ways. It is smaller in size and has only three toes on the hind legs, fewer teeth, a small tail, complex stomach, and musk or scent glands on the rump. Peccaries are about 3 feet long and stand about 20 inches at the shoulder. They can weigh up to 65 pounds but generally weigh about 35 to 40 pounds. They are blackish brown in color with a dirty yellow-brown mixed with white on the flanks. There is also a lighter stripe around the shoulders like a faint collar, hence the name. They will eat almost anything, vegetable or animal, but generally feed on roots, grain and fruit. They have litters of one or two young almost any time of year, usually born in a cave or hollow log. They have short sharp tusks and run in small herds of perhaps a dozen. While they will, and often do, fight viciously if threatened, they will also escape into dens if possible. There are peccaries in Central America and Mexico which are white-lipped and so named. These prefer forests and run in herds of up to 200, and can be dangerous. Natural enemies are the jaguar, bobcat, wolf, coyote and ocelot. Man also hunts the peccary for its hide and meat which is excellent.

Cottontail Rabbit Sylvilagus floridanus

The cottontail's real name is the eastern cottontail rabbit, although it can be found in some of the western parts of the country as well, wherever there is thick brush and brier patches in which it can hide. Its close relatives, the desert cottontail and brush rabbit, are found in the western portions of the United States and down into Mexico. All are true rabbits—that is, their young are born blind and hairless. Some animals which we call rabbits are actually hares. Their young are born fully furred and with their eyes open. The cottontail have from two to eight little, helpless young any time from early spring to late summer. Although rabbits usually live for about 5 years, some have been known to live for as long as 13 years. They feed on grass, soft plants, vegetables, flowers, and in winter various kinds of bark. They live in hollow logs and in burrows underground. The nest in which the young are born is lined with soft fur from the mother's body. Cottontails are generally dark brown with a lighter underside, a white eye circle, and a white tail—what there is of it. Desert cottontails are, however, lighter in color for better protection. The fur on the legs and feet is shorter and finer than that on the body. Other species of cottontail rabbits include the marsh rabbit, swamp rabbit and little pygmy rabbit. All are basically the same with minor differences in size, color and range.

Jackrabbit Lepus californicus

There are several species of these long-eared chaps leaping around our western states. All of them are famous for their long ears and great leaps, some covering as much as 20 feet at a jump and racing along at 45 mph. These rabbits (actually hares) are found west of the Mississippi in barren areas where they feed upon almost any kind of vegetation, with a special appetite for alfalfa and grain. They can get along with very little water and will also browse on bark, twigs, and any kind of soft plant that is handy. They live in burrows and have frequent litters of from one to six youngsters. The young hares are born fully furred and with eyes open and are able to run in an hour or so. "Jacks" can be found from lower Canada down into Mexico, and they form the main food supply of coyotes and similar predators. Some species of jackrabbits weigh as much as 11 pounds but generally our western species weigh 7 or 8 pounds. When startled, a jack will leap high in the air to see where the danger is before dashing away. Coyotes hunt these small game animals in relays, often driving them close to another coyote waiting in ambush.

Snowshoe Rabbit Lepus americanus

This "white rabbit" really isn't a rabbit, nor is it always white, at least all of the time. Actually it can be kept from turning white at all with a little artificial light. This small game animal is the varying hare found in Canada and the colder areas of the United States. It is called a snowshoe rabbit because it has long paws furred on both sides for better traction on snow and ice. It is called a varying hare because it is a hare rather than a rabbit, and because its color varies with the cold and length of day. In summer it is dark brown with a lighter underside, but as days grow shorter and temperature falls, this white extends up along the sides until the animal is all white for winter camouflage. If one of these rabbits is exposed to artificial light for 18 hours a day it does not change to white at all, even in cold temperatures, and a white one can be changed back to the brown of summer by exposure to artificial light to simulate longer days. They weigh about 4 pounds and eat barks and twigs almost exclusively. They are preyed upon by bobcats, lynx, foxes, wolves, marten, wolverines, and similar predators. Their population rises and falls in periods of 10 years, along with that of their enemies. They do not burrow, but den up in hollow logs or small caves. They usually have three or four youngsters (ten is the maximum) in late spring or summer.

Virginia Opossum Didelphis virginiana

This ratlike four-legged relic of prehistoric times is America's only pouched animal. The youngsters are born in two litters a year and each litter may number up to twenty! When born, the young opossums are smaller than a honeybee. They measure only ½ inch long and weigh 1/270 ounce. They crawl through the mother's hair into the pouch on her abdomen where her nipples are located. The first eleven to thirteen begin to feed and do not let go. The rest, unable to find nourishment, die. This unique animal is found over most of eastern United States and down into Mexico. There are several small species in South America, some as small as rats and mice. The opossum has grayish to white coarse fur, a bare pinkish tail and black feet. Its face is white, the nose pink and the ears black areas. Opossums live on insects, fruit, eggs, roots, birds, small mammals, crayfish, carrion and poultry. They weigh up to about 14 pounds and are generally slow-moving. When threatened, they may run away, hide, hiss and bare their teeth, actually fight, or play dead. This latter is interesting to see, for they are great actors. If left alone, they soon "revive" and amble off. They are night people, and climb well, using their prehensile tails as a third hand to climb with. (Prehensile means adapted for reaching and holding onto something.) They spend their days in a burrow or hollow tree.

Bobcat Lynx rufus

The bobcat, whose photo I took for the cover, is also known as the wildcat and bay lynx. This animal is about the same size as the lynx opposite but can be identified by the shorter fur, smaller ear tufts, smaller feet and shorter sideburns on the cheeks. Bobcats range over much of the continent of North America except in what has been called the "corn belt." They are found in both northern wilderness areas and Florida's semitropical Everglades and can even be found within 50 miles of New York's Times Square. Like the lynx, they measure about 3 feet long, including a 6-inch tail, and stand about 23 inches at the shoulder. They feed on rodents, rabbits, birds and occasionally small or injured deer and domestic animals. They have about four kittens in the spring and their dens are in caves and occasionally hollow logs. Their cries are catlike squalls, mewings and sometimes a real, startling screech. They are found in open country, thick brush, swamps and almost any place that food can be found in abundance. The youngsters stay with their parents for about a year and then go off on their own. They live to be about 15 years old. Like the lynx, they are rarely seen by man.

Canada Lynx Lynx canadensis

If you only caught a glimpse of this small cat in the woods, you could easily mistake it for a bobcat. Their maximum weight is about the same, up to 40 pounds, but the Canadian lynx appears larger owing to its longer hair, larger feet and tufted ears. The tail of the lynx is black-tipped but not barred as is that of the bobcat. The coat is generally gray with brown mottlings, and usually lighter in color than the bobcat's. The lynx feeds upon small animals such as rabbits, mice and occasionally birds, and serves as a balance to the rabbit population. The lynx population, confined to the northern parts of the North American continent, fluctuates with the 7- to 10-year cycle of the snowshoe rabbit population, its principal diet. The lynx can swim well if need be. One of its identifying marks is its "sideburns" of thick hair below its cheeks. Note, in the photo, the tufted ears and these side whiskers. The one to four kittens are heavily spotted when born, in a den in the rocks in late spring. Lynx cries are a mixture of squalls and other catlike noises with an occasional hair-raising screech. The kittens, whose noises I have taped in Canada, have an almost birdlike chirp.

Kinkajou Potos flavus

From Mexico well down into South America the kinkajou scampers through the trees like a monkey, using its prehensile tail like an extra hand to grasp branches as it darts about. In Mexico it is sometimes called a "monkey lion" because of its ability to use its tail like a monkey. It is most unusual for a carnivore to have a prehensile tail. The kinkajou has a body about a foot long and a tail almost twice this in length. Its color is a dark brown or golden brown and its fur is soft and woolly. The eyes are large and soft and ears are small. The kinkajou is extremely agile. It uses its nimble front paws to carry food to its mouth. Its food is mainly soft fruit, which it tears open and then uses its mobile tongue to reach. It will also eat insects, small mammals and small birds. It has from two to four young which are born covered with soft black fur. At 7 weeks they too can hang by their tails. They live to almost 20 years. They are almost entirely nocturnal, spending the daytime sleeping in a hollow tree.

Nine-banded Armadillo Dasypus novemcinctus

This armor-plated animal is found from our southern states all the way down into Argentina, where it is joined by others of its species. It has nine bands of scales between its front armor and its rear section of armor, hence its name. These plates are composed of bony material, and in some species cover the entire head. These animals are about 28 inches long and weigh up to about 15 pounds. In spite of their ungainly look and slow walk, they can swim well and walk safely along the bottom of a stream or body of water, staying submerged for as long as six minutes if need be. They feed on insects, snakes, lizards and also fruit and vegetables and occasionally poultry. They damage crops and, as they sometimes travel in groups of over 50, can wreck a garden in short order. They live in burrows. As many as 15 animals, generally all of one sex, may live in the same burrow. They have from four to eight young at a time, all of one sex. They are found from sea level up to 10,000 feet in elevation. This animal is often called the Texas armadillo as he is very abundant in that state.

Giant and Six-banded Armadillos

Priodontes giganteus and Dasypus sexcinctus

Several species of armadillos are found in Central and South America. The photo shows the giant armadillo found in Brazilian forests, left, and the little six-banded armadillo found in Paraguay and Brazil. The giant armadillo measures over 5 feet long while the little one shown with him is only a foot and a half in length. The giant armadillo feeds almost exclusively on termites. Its third toe ends in a unusually large claw which it uses to rip open termite nests. It has 12 or 13 bands along its back and twice as many teeth as other types of armadillos. The little six-banded armadillo has a short tail, small ears and quite a broad head compared with the long slender heads of the nine-banded armadillo. Almost all of these armor-plated animals can roll themselves up so that their soft underparts are protected with armor against an attacker. One tiny armadillo is only about 6 inches long and is covered with about 20 pink horny plates and soft white fur. It is called the fairy armadillo and looks like a toy. This cute little animal is found in western Argentina and lives underground most of the time.

Agouti Dasyprocta aguti

There are several species of these little game animals and all of them are considered good eating by both predators and man. They are chiefly nocturnal, spending their days in holes in the ground or hollows in trees. They weigh about 5 pounds and are about the size of a big cottontail rabbit. Their fur is a sleek golden or reddish brown with lighter areas on the underside, throat and muzzle. They have very short tails. The young are born almost any time of year and number from four to six. Families remain together for some time. Agoutis live for about 10 years. They feed on fruit and vegetables and often become pests where there are gardens. One way the natives hunt these animals is to find their burrows and then, from hiding, toss stones into the air so they fall near the burrows. The animals think that fruit has fallen and come out to get it and so are taken. Their front feet have five toes and the hind feet three, with huge claws. They trot slowly or run in a series of fast jumps so they look as if they were galloping. They will jump into water if closely pursued and can swim well, but cannot dive. Agoutis range from southern Mexico down into South America.

Capybara Hydrochoerus capybara

The family of rodents includes species ranging from the tiny field mouse to this, the largest living rodent, the capybara found in South America. It lives in the lakes, marshes and swamps east of the foothills of the Andes Mountains. These huge rodents weigh as much as 120 pounds! They are 4 feet long and stand 21 inches at the shoulder. All of their feet are webbed, for they spend most of their lives in and around water feeding on vegetable matter and water plants. They run in small bands or family groups and will take to the water if pursued, swimming long distances underwater to escape. They can stay beneath the surface for several minutes at a time and their young take readily to the water as soon as they can get about. The young are born in litters of from two to eight at almost any time of the year, as are most young born in the tropics, where there are no real seasons. The color of the capybara is brown above and yellowish brown on the underparts. Its fur is thin, coarse and long. The head is broad and the muzzle thick and blunt. The eyes and ears look small for the size of the animal. Capybaras live to be about 10 years old.

Tree Porcupine Coendou prehensilis

This odd-looking animal with the unusual prehensile tail spends most of its time in the trees where it moves slowly about feeding on fruits, leaves and tender bark and twigs. It often spends a day or more in a particularly attractive tree. The long tail is unique in that it has stiff bristles at the root to aid in gripping smooth tree trunks. The spines of this porcupine are short and stiff, rather than long and flexible like those of some of our own more familiar "porkies." This tree porcupine is practically hairless but has plenty of the short deadly "quills" to give it protection. It is about 3 feet long and may reach a weight of from 25 to 30 pounds. It generally has one youngster at a time with an occasional set of twins. It has only four toes on its hind feet, but it has a broad fleshy pad like a palm which it uses along with its toes to grip tree branches when climbing. The front feet have five toes with claws. It dens up in holes in trees although it often sleeps curled up in a broad tree crotch. Not much is known of its habits.

Northern Giant Otter

Pteronura brasiliensis brasiliensis

This huge aquatic animal is found throughout much of the Amazon basin of South America. It resembles our own river otter but is far larger, running to well over 6 feet in length compared with the 4-foot length of our own species. It also has a differently shaped tail. The tail of our otter is round and tapered, while the tail of this big fellow is flattened laterally, something like that of the beaver, but furred. All four feet of this animal are webbed, unlike the river otter which has only the hind feet webbed, and it is an expert swimmer. It digs dens along the riverbanks and feeds on fish, frogs and small mammals. The color of this sleek swimmer is a dark reddish brown with light chin, throat and edge of mouth. The very small ears are set well back and it has a short broad muzzle like that of our own otters. This otter generally has only one litter a year and the young usually number from one to four. Not much is known about the habits of this elusive animal, also known as the giant Brazilian otter.

Chinchilla Chinchilla laniger

Various species of the chinchilla are to be found all through the Peruvian Andes. These little animals are noted for their luxurious fur which has more fibers per square inch than any other animal fur. They prefer desert or semidesert areas and rocky mountainsides. They are about 10 inches long with a bushy tail of about the same length. The fur is soft silvery gray with lighter legs and feet. The eyes and ears are large, and the tail has an upward sweep at the end. They are said to mate for life and have two or three litters of young a year. The litters average from a single offspring to as many as four, born in a den or burrow in the ground. They frequently take dust baths in fine dry sand, apparently to keep their fur clean and free from vermin. At the beginning of the century they were almost trapped into extinction but now strict laws protect them. They are said to live about 10 years. Some species are found as high as 17,000 feet up in the mountains. Chinchillas feed on grass and other vegetation and few insects. Many give sharp warning whistles in time of danger.

Jaguarundi Herpailurus jaguarundi

There are two distinct color phases of this species of small feline, a rusty-red phase and an iron-gray phase. Neither is spotted. They are found from Paraguay northward through Central America and Mexico into some of our southwestern states. The jaguarundi is also known as the eyra, or otter cat, and undoubtedly ranges in many places where it is unknown because of its furtive and elusive ways. It is about 50 inches long and it stands about a foot high at the shoulder. It weighs up to 20 pounds and lives on small animals, birds, reptiles, frogs, insects and some fish. It makes its den in small caves or even a hollow log where it has its young. The young may be of either color phase. This little South American cat spends much of its time in or near water. It is a fine swimmer and, unlike most cats, enjoys the water, where it catches much of its foods.

Ocelot Felis pardalis

One of the sleekest and most elusive small game cats of the Americas is the ocelot. This little wildcat ranges from the southern United States down into Paraguay, and it is believed that at one time it ranged as far north as Ohio. Ocelots have a total length of only 3 feet including a 15-inch tail, but they are so well proportioned that they might be taken for a larger animal. They weigh about 35 pounds and are grayish yellow with large black-edged spots. The ears are black and upper cheeks white. The long tail is ringed, and helps to balance the animal as it leaps and climbs. They are carnivores, hunting birds, amphibians, monkeys, kids, young pigs, lambs and other animals. They will not attack man but are terrific fighters if cornered. They hunt mostly after dark, and frequently as a pair, keeping in touch by low mewing noises. They mate at almost any time. The kittens are born in dens in rocks or occasionally a hollow log. There are only one or two in each litter, usually twins. Ocelots are fine climbers and spend much time in the trees looking for monkeys. They are also known as tiger cat, painted leopard and labba tiger. A similar small wildcat is the margay, only 18 inches long including its 8-inch tail. The margay ranges from Mexico down into Peru, and is marked with black lines and bands against a grayish-yellow color.

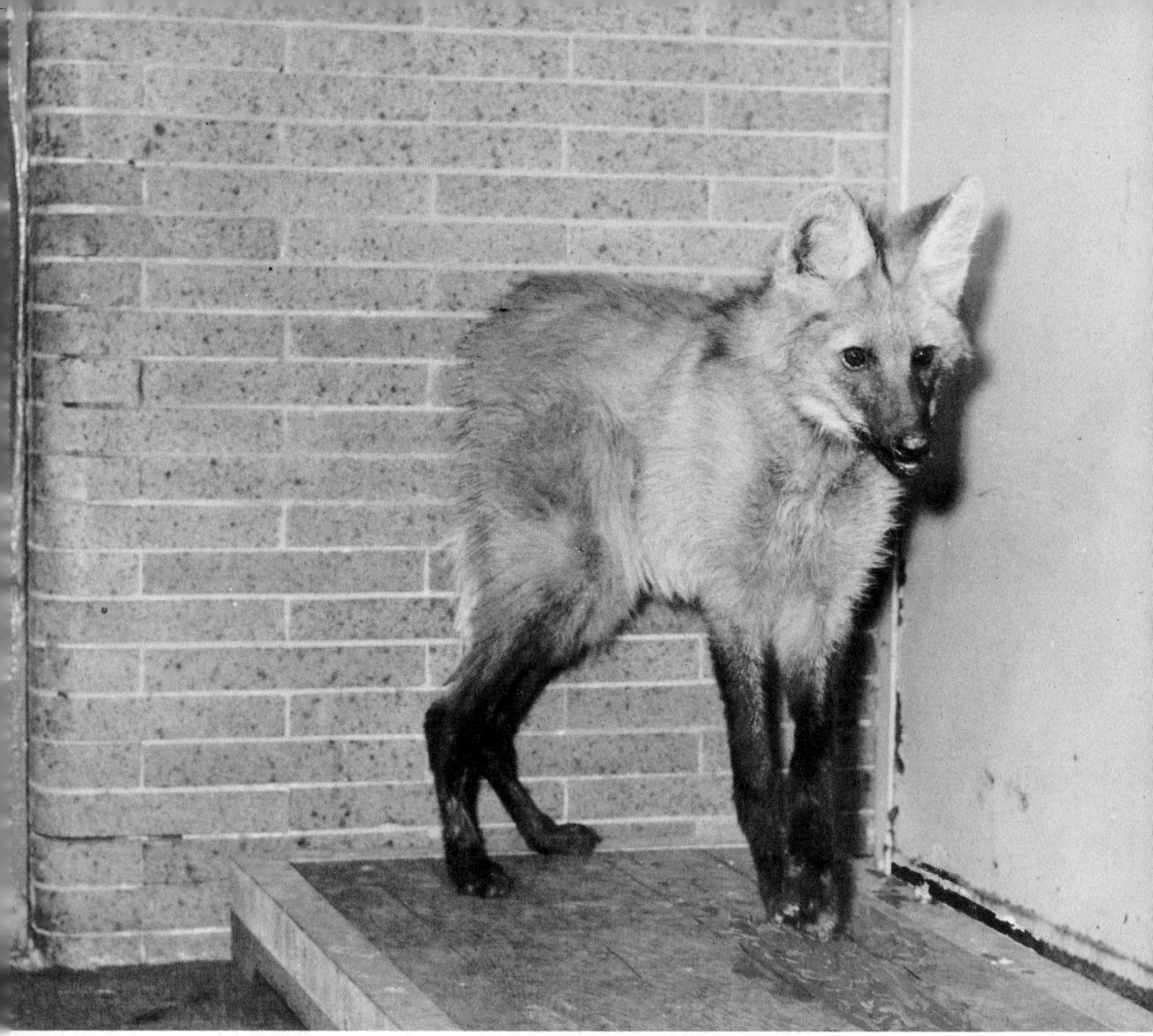

Maned Wolf Chrysocyon jubatus

You may think this animal looks like a mixed-up affair—its legs too long and too close together, the neck far too short, the ears too large and the fur a sort of collection of odds and ends. Actually the maned wolf, found in the Amazon basin, Paraguay and northern Argentina, is a pretty efficient animal. It lives in forests and clearings and hunts for rodents, birds and insects. It stands nearly 30 inches at the shoulder and weighs up to about 25 pounds. Including its tail it is about 5 feet long. Its color is approximately that of the red fox, a reddish brown all over with darker feet and legs. It has a dark mane on top of its shoulders and neck, hence the name. The underside and throat are lighter, as are the insides of its ears. This animal is seldom seen, but is frequently heard yapping. It sounds somewhat like our coyotes. It has been reported that the maned wolf seldom does any digging, which is unusual for a canine, and that it lives in caves. Very little is really known about this interesting "wolf."

Azara's Dog Dusicyon gymnocercus

This animal may look like a cross between a dog and a fox, but actually it is classed as a jackal. It has shorter legs than a coyote and is shaggier than a fox. It stands about 16 inches at the shoulder and is about 3 ½ feet long including the tail. Azara's dog is generally nocturnal, hunting for its food by night. It feeds on small mammals, poultry if it can find any, and occasionally birds. Its color is a yellowish gray with lighter legs and feet. The ears are quite large and erect, and the tip of the bushy tail is darker. This animal uses a hollow log or small cave for a den. Not much is known about the habits of these "dogs" but, being members of the jackal clan, they undoubtedly have from three to six puppies in a litter and probably live for about 14 years.

Round-eared Dog Atelocynus microtis

This animal, which looks very little like a dog, is found along the upper Amazon River in South America. It is also known as the short-eared dog. It is a dark reddish brown all over but its feet and legs are darker than the rest of its body. The tail is so long that it touches the ground when the animal lowers it. The ears, unlike those of foxes, wolves and jackals, are short, rounded and close to the head. It stands about a foot high at the shoulder and is about 3 feet long. Its fur is smooth and short, more like that of a hound than a fox or coyote. The eyes are quite large and the muzzle is slender and pointed. The hind legs are longer than the front. It is usually nocturnal, doing most of its hunting at night. It feeds on small rodents, birds and occasionally eggs and some insects. Not much is known about its habits as it is very shy and elusive. Its den is usually found in a small cave, hollow log or occasionally in a hole taken over from some other animal.

Ecuadorian Wild Dog Dusicyon culpaeus reisii

Not much is known about the habits of this little foxlike animal from the Andes of Ecuador. It looks very much like a small coyote or our gray fox. Its fur is a brownish gray and quite shaggy. The ears are large and well furred. The tip of the tail is darker, there are light spots over each eye and the muzzle is lighter. It stands 15 inches at the shoulder and measures about 3 feet in length. It does most of its hunting by night although it is often active in the daytime. It feeds on small mammals, some insects and birds when it can catch them on the ground or nesting. Its den is among the rocks or dug under tree roots for better protection. Its voice is a yapping bark like that of the round-eared dog. The wild dog occasionally hunts with its mate.

Bush Dog Speothos venaticus

Many think this odd-looking little "dog" is a relic from some early canine species which has been lost in history. It resembles the short-legged dachshund but has a very short and rather bushy tail. Its hair is short and coarse and its ears are short and rounded. It stands about 9 inches tall and is about 2 feet long. Its weight is about 8 to 12 pounds. The pinkish lower lip usually shows, and the eyes, small and reddish brown, often appear watery as if from crying. It is a sort of sad-looking little animal, but a very efficient hunter and den digger. The bush dogs' dens or burrows are well constructed. They are meat eaters and generally nocturnal, coming out at night to hunt for small mammals, birds and insects. Their voice is quite unusual, for it includes all sorts of birdlike chirps, whistles, odd clicking sounds and a low mumble. They are usually making some sort of noise as they go about their hunting.

Tamandua Tamandua tetradactyla

Excluding the great anteater (*Myrmecophaga jubata*), which is hardly small game, there are several smaller anteaters which can be mentioned. The tamandua, shown above, ranges from Central America south to northern Argentina. It is about 4 feet long and tawny buff in color with black patches and markings. Its hair is relatively short. The tail is long and prehensile for grasping branches as it climbs about the trees in search of food. Its muzzle is long and tapering and its tongue is coated with a sticky substance for collecting the ants it feeds upon. It generally finds the ants it lives on in trees but its powerful claws can rip open their nests wherever it finds them. The tamandua has only one young and this small youngster is carried about clinging to its mother's tail until able to get about on its own. Another, much smaller anteater, the little or two-toed anteater (*Cyclopes didactylus*), ranges from Mexico to Bolivia and is only 15 inches long. It too lives in trees and feeds on ants.

Three-toed Sloth Bradypus tridactylus

The sloths are a unique form of small game. They spend almost all their lives upside down. They are very slow-moving and climb about the trees in which they live, hand over foot with the aid of long curved claws that act as hanging hooks. The three-toed sloth has three of these hooks on the front feet and four on the hind feet. The toes are enclosed in a common skin so the feet look like hairy pads armed with hooks. The front legs are longer than the rear. The head is short and broad. These animals are about 20 inches long. The neck and joints of the limbs are very flexible so they can look in all directions and turn their limbs to reach out in any direction. They have long, quite stiff hair which is grayish or brownish in color, but appears green because grooves in the hair are lined with tiny green algae. Some have a small patch of black or orange between their shoulders. They feed exclusively on the leaves and fruit of the Cecropia tree. They have a single young which clings to the body of its mother. Sloths are almost helpless on the ground and move at the speed of one mile in 6½ hours! They can swim if need be, but poorly. Their natural enemy is the jaguar. Their senses of sight, hearing and taste all are poor. Sloths live alone except at mating time.

Two-toed Sloth Choloepus didactylus

Compared with the three-toed sloth on the opposite page, the two-toed sloth is quite an athlete, for it can actually walk on the ground. This species of sloth has only two hooks on its front feet, one less than its relative, but it has four on its hind feet. It can move twice as fast as the three-toed sloth, and on the ground can actually stand up on all four legs with its body clear of the ground. In contrast, the three-toed sloth lies flat on the ground unable to raise its body, and drags itself along using its claws as hooks stuck into the ground. The two-toed sloth has limbs of equal length, but lacks a tail, while the three-toed fellow has a little stump of a tail. The two-toed sloth in captivity will eat a variety of such things as fruit, vegetables and bread and milk, while the three-toed variety will still eat only the stems, buds, and leaves of the Cecropia tree. This animal's limbs and neck are very limber as with other sloths. Like them, it has only one young at a time. The young cling to the body of the mother as she moves about the trees. The hair of all sloths grows in opposite directions to that of other animals so that while upside down it will shed the rain. This sloth and the three-toed sloth opposite, range from Honduras south to the Amazon river.

Tayra Galera barbara

This otterlike small game can be found from Mexico through Central America down into Argentina, especially in forests and thick grasslands. The tayra's length is 3 ½ feet, of which half is a long flexible tail. Its fur is a dark brown with a lighter spot on its chest. The head and neck are gray, but the color is often variable. Tayras often hunt in packs of up to 20 at a time, scouring the ground for rodents, birds and eggs. They are mainly nocturnal, but may be active up to midday, spending the rest of the daylight hours in a hollow tree, in a shelter under a ledge, or in an armadillo's abandoned den. They are agile and curious, poking their noses into any crack or opening for food. They have two young at a time, but not much more is known about their habits.